2   3   4   5   6   7   8   9   10

More Easy Answers

by Joyce Richards

Illustrated by Susan Perl

Platt and Munk, Publishers/New York

Do flowers grow everywhere?

There are over 250,000 different types of flowers. They grow almost everywhere in the world, in almost every kind of climate.

Some flowers, like orchids, grow deep in jungles. Some, like water

lilies, float on top of ponds. Some, like cactus flowers, grow in the driest, sandiest deserts. Other flowers, like buttercups and daisies, dandelions and Queen Anne's lace, grow almost everywhere.

The only places flowers don't grow are in the middle of the ocean and in the coldest, iciest parts of the North and South Poles.

What is sand?

Sand is bits of rock and minerals and shells and coral that have been ground into tiny grains by wind, rain, waves, or freezing weather. Beaches and deserts are made of sand. There is sand at the bottom of the ocean and in deep lakes. Where else is there sand? In sandboxes!

What are valentines?

Valentines are cards or messages or gifts to send to friends on St. Valentine's Day, which falls on February 14th each year.

St. Valentine's Day is a day for showing affection. People have been celebrating it for hundreds of years by exchanging candy, cards, or flowers.

What is the Liberty Bell?

The Liberty Bell is a big bell that weighs over 2000 pounds. It is almost as heavy as a small car. This bell is a famous symbol of America's freedom. That is because it was rung to celebrate the independence of the United States in July, 1776.

In 1835 the bell was rung for the last time. It cracked then and broke. The crack in its side is still seen today by the millions of people who visit the Liberty Bell in Philadelphia, where it is kept in its own building.

How do ducks swim?

The duck is a very strong swimmer. Unlike most birds, it has widespread webbed feet that work like paddles, pushing the water back and its body forward with each stroke. On land it looks clumsy and walks with a funny waddle, but in the water it moves smoothly and swiftly.

The duck also has a special gland near its tail that gives off oil and makes its feathers waterproof. This oil, which it spreads over its feathers with its bill, helps keep it afloat.

How high is the sky?

The sky is so high it is impossible to measure. The highest clouds you can see are about 50 miles up. They are in a part of the sky called the "atmosphere," which goes up about 600 miles. Beyond the atmosphere, nobody knows how high the sky is.

We do know that the sun is 93 million miles away. We also know the nearest star we can see at night is 49 trillion miles away. But we will never know exactly how high the sky is.

What's the biggest animal in the world?

The biggest animal in the world lives in the ocean. You might think it is a fish, but it is not. It is the blue whale, and it is the biggest animal that ever lived. It is even bigger than the diplodocus, the largest dinosaur.

A grown-up blue whale can be over 100 feet long. A baby blue whale, just one day old, can be as long as 25 feet. But as big as blue whales are, they are as gentle as tiny kittens.

What good are earthworms?

Earthworms are very valuable to people. Without them we might not have plants and vegetables.

As earthworms slide and wiggle through the earth, they form long round tunnels that let air and water flow down to the plant roots and help prevent the soil from getting hard and dry.

At night, earthworms come up to the surface to eat tiny bits of leaves, leaving behind droppings, called "castings." These castings help fertilize the top soil.

Who was Mother Goose?

Nobody knows whether Mother Goose, the old lady who told nursery rhymes, was a real person or not. Some people think she was the mother of a great emperor named Charlemagne. This lady was called Queen Goosefoot and was known for telling fabulous tales.

The first book of stories with Mother Goose's name on them was published in France in 1697. Since then, thousands of Mother Goose books of rhymes and jingles and nonsense songs have been written.

Why do we have to eat vegetables?

Vegetables give us much of the vitamins, minerals, and protein we need to grow up strong and healthy. Some help make our eyes stronger. Some help strengthen our gums and teeth. Some help make

our bones firm and our bodies sturdy. It is possible that eating vegetables every day can even make us happier.

How many kinds of pets are there?

There are probably as many kinds of pets as there are animals and birds and fish and insects. That's because almost anything that crawls or flies or swims or squirms has been somebody's pet at some time.

The most popular pets are dogs, cats, fish, and canaries. But in Mexico children make pets of fleas. In Japan they sometimes train mice to dance. And in India children have tamed everything from crickets to elephants.